CASTAWAY SQUADRON

BY THE SPRING OF 1943 THE BITTERLY-FOUGHT BATTLE OF THE ATLANTIC WAS AT ITS HEIGHT, AND WHILE SOME CONVOYS MADE THE OCEAN CROSSING UNDETECTED AND UNSCATHED OTHERS WERE NOT SO FORTUNATE — ESPECIALLY ONE WHICH WAS SPOTTED BY A LURKING U-BOAT LESS THAN A DAY INTO ITS VOYAGE.

STORY
ALAN HEBDEN

ART
CARLOS PINO

COVER
CARLOS PINO

SIGNAL H.Q. EASTBOUND CONVOY CONTACTED AT THIS LOCATION. APPROXIMATELY FORTY MERCHANT SHIPS AND NO MORE THAN FIVE NAVY ESCORTS. WILL PROCEED TO SHADOW IT.

THE NEWS WAS FLASHED TO THE U-BOATS' OPERATIONAL HEADQUARTERS IN LORIENT ON THE FRENCH COAST. IT WAS JUST WHAT THE GERMAN COMMANDING OFFICER HAD BEEN WAITING FOR.

IN TWO DAYS THE CONVOY WILL BE BEYOND THE RANGE OF LAND-BASED AIR COVER. GIVE THE ORDER FOR A WOLF PACK TO ASSEMBLE IN THAT AREA. I WANT AS MANY ALLIED SHIPS SUNK AS POSSIBLE!

JAWOHL, HERR ADMIRAL!

ALTHOUGH THE GERMAN NAVY'S SIGNAL ENCRYPTION REMAINED UNBROKEN THROUGHOUT THE WAR, IT DID NOT NEED A CODEBREAKER TO TELL THE BRITISH THAT THE RESULTING FLURRY OF SIGNALS, PICKED UP BY A CHAIN OF TRACKING STATIONS, SPELT BIG TROUBLE.

THE PATTERN OF SIGNALS SAYS IT ALL. THERE'S DEFINITELY A WOLF PACK ASSEMBLING IN MID-OCEAN.

I'LL INFORM THE ADMIRALTY IMMEDIATELY.

THE ESCORTS DID THEIR BEST, BUT FORCED TO STICK CLOSE TO THE CONVOY THEY RARELY HAD A CHANCE TO FOLLOW UP ON ANY SONAR CONTACT.

WE'VE GOT A CONTACT BEARING OH-NINE-FIVE, SKIPPER.

LET IT GO. WE CAN'T GO CHASING ANYTHING AT THE MOMENT.

THE U-BOAT SKIPPERS KNEW THIS AS WELL, AND AS SOON AS AN ESCORT MOVED ON THEY TURNED BACK TO LAUNCH ANOTHER ATTACK.

LOOK OUT. AAARGH!

IF EVER THERE WAS A CASE FOR ORDERING THE CONVOY TO SCATTER, THAT WAS IT, BUT NO AMOUNT OF PLEADING COULD CHANGE THE CONVOY COMMANDER'S MIND.

WE CAN'T GO ON LOSING SHIPS LIKE THIS, SKIPPER. AT LEAST IF IT'S EVERY SHIP FOR HERSELF, SOME WILL ESCAPE.

WE MAINTAIN COURSE AND SHAPE, NUMBER ONE. THAT'S AN ORDER!

IT WAS NOT ONLY THE CONVOY COMMANDER'S DEPUTY WHO WAS WORRIED. UP AND DOWN THE LINES OF SHIPS THE MERCHANT MASTERS WERE BECOMING INCREASINGLY CONCERNED.

THE STRACKEN'S BEEN HIT, SKIPPER.

THIS IS INTOLERABLE! IF THE CONVOY COMMANDER THINKS WE'RE GOING TO GO LIKE SHEEP TO THE SLAUGHTER, HE CAN THINK AGAIN, SIGNAL OUR NEAREST NEIGHBOURS.

BEFORE LONG SIGNAL LAMPS WERE FLASHING URGENTLY BETWEEN THE MERCHANT SHIPS. THEY WERE ALL AGREED ON ONE THING, THAT THIS COULD NOT GO ON. IT WAS TIME TO TAKE THE LAW INTO THEIR OWN HANDS.

IN EXACTLY FIVE MINUTES WE BEGIN TO SCATTER.

AGREED. WHAT'S THE CONVOY COMMANDER GOING TO DO? OPEN FIRE ON US?

NO-ONE WOULD EVER KNOW WHAT MIGHT HAVE HAPPENED BECAUSE LESS THAN A MINUTE BEFORE THE MERCHANT SHIPS ACTED, A LOOK-OUT YELLED INCREDULOUSLY.

FIGHTER AIRCRAFT COMING OUR WAY!

WHAT? WHERE DID THEY COME FROM?

THE NEW ARRIVALS WERE BRITISH SUPERMARINE SEAFIRE ESCORTS.

THE SEAFIRES TOOK UP PATROL POSITIONS AROUND THE CONVOY, FORCING THE U-BOATS TO SUBMERGE COMPLETELY, WHICH MEANT THEY COULD NO LONGER KEEP UP WITH THE CONVOY.

THAT'S A SIGHT FOR SORE EYES.

AND LOOK WHAT'S COMING!

WHAT THE DELIGHTED MERCHANT SEAMEN SAW WAS THE ARRIVAL ON THE SCENE OF A POTENT NEW WEAPON AGAINST THE U-BOATS KNOWN AS A CONVOY SUPPORT GROUP. LED BY THE ESCORT CARRIER H.M.S. GROWLER, ACCOMPANIED BY A FAST DESTROYER AND TWO FRIGATES, ALL WERE PURPOSE-BUILT, ANTI-SUBMARINE WARFARE VESSELS WITH HIGHLY-TRAINED CREWS TO MATCH.

GROWLER TO SUPPORT GROUP, THE SEAFIRES HAVE LOCATED AT LEAST FOUR U-BOATS. BREAK OFF AND HUNT THEM DOWN!

ROGER, SKIPPER!

FOR THE U-BOATS THE NIGHTMARE WAS ONLY JUST BEGINNING. THE NEW HUNTER-KILLERS WERE NOT TIED TO THE CONVOY AS THE ESCORTS WERE. ONCE THEY MADE CONTACT THEY WOULD PURSUE THEIR PREY FOR AS LONG AS IT TOOK TO FINISH THEM OFF, USING THE LATEST FORWARD-FIRING DEPTH CHARGES THAT GAVE MUCH GREATER ACCURACY.

THERE GOES ANOTHER ONE!

AIEE!

FOR THE CONVOY COMMANDER IT HAD BEEN A CLOSE RUN THING, BUT NOW HE COULD EXPLAIN HIS PREVIOUS SILENCE.

SIGNAL ALL SHIPS, NUMBER ONE. APOLOGISE FOR KEEPING THEM IN THE DARK, BUT WE COULDN'T RISK THE WOLF PACK GETTING WIND OF THE SUPPORT GROUP'S APPROACH AND SCATTERING BEFORE IT ARRIVED.

AS THE CONVOY SAILED ON, THE BROKEN WOLF PACK FLED IN EVERY DIRECTION. UNFORTUNATELY FOR TWO OF THEM, THEY MADE THE MISTAKE OF GETTING TOO CLOSE, RESULTING IN A DISASTROUS COLLISION.

WE'VE HIT SOMETHING. AAARGH!

DONNER AND BLITZEN. UURGH!

AYE, AYE, SKIPPER!

AS THE U-BOAT MENACE FADED GROWLER WAS ORDERED TO CAPE TOWN, SOUTH AFRICA, TO UNDERGO A MUCH-NEEDED REFIT AND REST HER EXHAUSTED CREW AND AIRCREW.

SO THAT'S TABLE MOUNTAIN.

BEFORE THEY EMBARKED ON A MONTHS' LEAVE, CAPTAIN HURST HAD SOME FRESH INFORMATION TO PASS ON.

IT LOOKS LIKE WE'LL BE CARRYING ON TO THE FAR EAST WHEN GROWLER'S BEEN GIVEN A FRESH LICK OF PAINT.

IN THAT CASE THE JAPS HAD BETTER LOOK OUT!

REPORTING BACK AFTER THEIR LEAVE BOB AND JOHNNY WERE SURPRISED TO FIND GROWLER'S FLIGHT DECK FULL OF PARKED AIRCRAFT.

MARTLETS AS WELL AS SEAFIRES. WHAT'S GOING ON?

LET'S ASK THE CAPTAIN.

THEY FOUND CAPTAIN HURST ON THE BRIDGE AND DISCOVERED THAT GROWLER WAS BEING GIVEN A TEMPORARY NEW ROLE.

WE'RE TRANSPORTING THAT LOT TO AUSTRALIA TO BE DISTRIBUTED TO OTHER ESCORT CARRIERS.

IT ALSO MEANS WE WON'T BE ABLE TO FLY ANYTHING OFF THE DECK UNTIL WE GET THERE.

THE INDIAN OCEAN WAS REGARDED AS MUCH LESS DANGEROUS THAN THE ATLANTIC, SO THERE WAS NO NEED FOR CONVOYS. IN GROWLER'S CASE, SHE WAS BEING ACCOMPANIED BY AN AUSTRALIAN DESTROYER, H.M.S. GERALDTON.

NEXT STOP, MELBOURNE.

EVEN BEFORE TABLE MOUNTAIN HAD SLIPPED OUT OF SIGHT JOHNNY, SOMETHING OF A NATURAL-BORN SNOOPER, HAD MADE A FEW MORE DISCOVERIES ABOUT THEIR CARGO OF AIRCRAFT.

THEY'VE ALL HAD THEIR RADIOS STRIPPED OUT TO BE REPLACED BY MORE POWERFUL ONES WHEN WE REACH AUSTRALIA, AND THE SHIP'S AVIATION FUEL TANKS ARE PRACTICALLY EMPTY.

MAKES SENSE. NO POINT IN CARRYING FUEL YOU CAN'T USE.

AS AN ADDITIONAL PRECAUTION THE TWO SHIPS TOOK A MORE SOUTHERLY ROUTE AWAY FROM THE MAIN SHIPPING LANES AND INTO THE "ROARING FORTIES". AS IT WAS NOW MIDWINTER IN THE SOUTHERN HEMISPHERE, THESE BOISTEROUS WESTERLY WINDS QUICKLY LIVED UP TO THEIR NAME.

SILLY OF ME TO HAVE SUPPOSED THE INDIAN OCEAN WAS A BALMY TROPICAL SEA. THIS IS AS WILD AS IT EVER GETS IN THE NORTH ATLANTIC.

LOOK, IS THAT AN ISLAND OVER THERE?

THEY FETCHED SOME BINOCULARS FOR A BETTER LOOK. TO BOB'S SURPRISE, THE PASSING ISLAND SEEMED TO BE INHABITED ENTIRELY BY SHEEP.

ENOUGH SHEEP TO COUNT YOURSELF TO SLEEP EVERY NIGHT FOR A YEAR, BUT WHERE ARE THE PEOPLE?

ONE OF THE SHIP'S OFFICERS, A SOUTH AFRICAN FROM THE CAPE, WAS ABLE TO EXPLAIN EVERYTHING.

IT'S CALLED LOST ISLAND. IT WAS SETTLED FOR A TIME BY SHEEP FARMERS FROM THE CAPE.

WHY WOULD ANYBODY WANT TO RAISE SHEEP IN THE MIDDLE OF THE OCEAN, ESPECIALLY ONE AS WILD AS THIS?

THE OFFICER TOLD THEM THAT DURING THE 19TH CENTURY SAILING SHIPS WOULD TAKE ADVANTAGE OF THE PREVAILING WINDS TO MAKE A FAST CROSSING TO AUSTRALIA. AS THESE OFTEN TURNED INTO RAGING TEMPESTS SHIPS SOUGHT SAFE ANCHORAGE OFF LOST ISLAND TO RIDE OUT THE STORM.

WE'LL BE SAFE AND SOUND HERE, HOWEVER BAD IT GETS.

APART FROM THE SHELTER, SHIPS COULD ALSO REPLENISH THEIR WATER SUPPLIES FROM THE ISLAND. THEN ONE DAY A SAILOR, WHO CAME FROM A FARMING FAMILY IN THE CAPE, HAD AN IDEA AS HE GAZED AT THE ROUGH PASTURE.

THERE'S A FUTURE FOR SHEEP HERE. A VERY PROFITABLE ONE.

THE IDEA WAS A SIMPLE ONE, THAT SHEEP ON LOST ISLAND COULD PROVIDE FRESH MUTTON FOR PASSING SHIPS. AFTER BEING PAID OFF AT THE END OF THE VOYAGE THE SAILOR RECRUITED TWO YOUNG COUSINS AND BOUGHT A SMALL FLOCK OF SHEEP. A YEAR LATER THEY ALL LANDED ON THE ISLAND.

GET MOVING, MUTTON CHOPS. THIS IS YOUR NEW HOME!

THE BUSINESS THRIVED FOR MANY YEARS UNTIL IT WAS FINALLY KILLED OFF BY THE AGE OF STEAM, WHICH MEANT MOST SHIPS COULD SAIL SHORTER ROUTES WITHOUT WORRYING ABOUT THE WINDS. AS MANY SHEEP AS POSSIBLE WERE ROUNDED UP TO BE TAKEN BACK TO SOUTH AFRICA, BUT INEVITABLY SOME WERE LEFT BEHIND.

YOU'VE GOT THE PLACE TO YOURSELVES, MUTTON CHOPS. BEST OF LUCK.

WE'LL MISS THIS PLACE.

AND THAT WAS HOW THE LEGEND OF LOST ISLAND CAME TO BE. THE STORYTELLER HAD ONE LAST SNIPPET TO ADD, THOUGH.

THE ONE THING EVERYONE WHO'S LANDED THERE SINCE AGREES ON IS THAT THE LOST SHEEP PROVIDE THE TASTIEST MUTTON IN THE WHOLE WORLD.

PITY IT'S A THREE-THOUSAND MILE ROUND TRIP FROM THE CAPE TO COME AND TASTE IT.

A FEW MINUTES LATER, AFTER AN EXCHANGE OF SIGNALS THE GERALDTON HOOTED AND TURNED AWAY FROM THE GROWLER.

SHE'S LEAVING US. WHAT'S GOING ON?

I'LL FIND OUT.

HE WENT TO THE BRIDGE TO DISCOVER WHAT WAS HAPPENING.

THERE'VE BEEN SIGHTINGS OF A SMALL JAP TASK FORCE CLOSE TO THE MAIN SHIPPING CHANNELS TO THE NORTH. EVERY AVAILABLE SHIP'S BEEN CALLED IN TO JOIN THE HUNT.

SO WE'RE ON OUR WAY NOW.

SEVERAL HOURS LATER THEY RAN INTO ONE OF THE INFAMOUS STORMS, FORCING CREW AND AIRMEN ALIKE TO BRAVE THE ROARING WINDS AND HEAVY RAIN TO CHECK THE PLANES ON DECK WERE SAFELY TIED DOWN.

LAST THING WE NEED IS FOR SOME TO START BLOWING OVER. WE'D HAVE A DOZEN WRECKS BEFORE WE KNEW IT.

WHIPPED UP BY THE STORM, THE HEAVY SEAS ALSO PLAYED HAVOC WITH THE SHIP'S RADAR. BY THE TIME THE OPERATOR REALISED HE HAD A CONTACT ON HIS SCREEN IT WAS ALREADY QUITE CLOSE.

CONTACT BEARING ONE-OH-FIVE! TELL THE BRIDGE THERE'S ANOTHER SHIP OUT THERE, COMING OUR WAY.

CAPTAIN HURST REQUESTED AN IMMEDIATE IDENTIFICATION REQUEST OVER THE RADIO, BUT AFTER SEVERAL FUTILE ATTEMPTS THERE WAS NO REPLY.

SHE'S NOT ANSWERING, SIR.

GO TO FULL ALERT UNTIL WE GET A SIGHTING.

THOUGH THE JAPANESE CRUISER'S GUNS WERE OF SIMILAR SIZE, THEY WERE LONGER BARRELLED AND CONSEQUENTLY HAD SLIGHTLY GREATER RANGE. COUPLED WITH HER GREATER SPEED AND MANOEUVRABILITY, IT MEANT SHE COULD STAND OFF AND CONTINUE TO POUND THE ESCORT CARRIER WITH IMPUNITY.

FIRE ALL GUNS! SINK THE FOREIGN DEVILS!

OUR SHELLS ARE FALLING SHORT!

IT WAS GLARINGLY APPARENT THAT GROWLER WAS DOOMED UNLESS SOMETHING CHANGED, AND BOB KNEW JUST WHAT IT HAD TO BE AS HE CONTACTED HURST OVER THE INTERCOM.

WE'VE GOT TO ARM AND FUEL THE SQUADRON'S SEAFIRES. IT'S OUR ONLY HOPE.

BUT HOW ARE YOU GOING TO TAKE OFF?

THERE WAS WORSE TO COME. ONE OF THE SHELLS HAD EXPLODED NEXT TO THE ENGINE ROOM, CAUSING WIDESPREAD DAMAGE. THE CHIEF ENGINEER PASSED ON THE BAD TIDINGS TO THE BRIDGE.

WE HAVE TO SHUT DOWN THE ENGINE, CAP'N. IF WE DON'T, THE WHOLE PLACE IS GOING TO EXPLODE.

GET THOSE FIRES OUT, MATES!

VERY WELL, CHIEF. KEEP ME INFORMED.

THE CAPTAIN COULD DO LITTLE BUT WATCH GRIM-FACED AS THE PLANES FLEW AWAY. WITHOUT RADIO CONTACT THERE WAS NO WAY OF TELLING THEM WHAT HAD HAPPENED.

A HOLED DECK AND THE SHIP ALL BUT DEAD IN THE WATER. WHATEVER HAPPENS, THEY WON'T BE ABLE TO LAND BACK HERE.

MEANWHILE, IT WAS THE CRUISER'S TURN TO FEEL THREATENED. AS HAD BEEN SHOWN MANY TIMES SINCE THE START OF THE WAR, ALL SHIPS, HOWEVER WELL-ARMED, WERE VULNERABLE TO AIR ATTACK.

ALL ANTI-AIRCRAFT BATTERIES OPEN FIRE!

DIE, BRITISHERS!

BEFORE THE FIRST BOMB WAS DROPPED ONE OF THE AIRCRAFT WAS DESTROYED. BOB LOOKED ON GRIMLY FROM HIS COCKPIT.

SMITHY'S BOUGHT IT.

AAIIEEGH!

ONLY THEN DID HE DISCOVER THAT THERE WOULD BE NO MORE LANDINGS ON GROWLER FOR THE IMMEDIATE FUTURE, WHICH POSED ANOTHER SERIOUS PROBLEM, ESPECIALLY IN AIRCRAFT WITHOUT RADIOS.

LOOKS LIKE WE'RE GOING TO HAVE TO DITCH ALONGSIDE OR BALE OUT. WAIT A SECOND, THOUGH . . . WHERE'S MY CHART?

THE CHART CONFIRMED WHAT BOB HAD BEEN THINKING, THAT THERE WAS ONE BIT OF LAND WITHIN REACH.

LOST ISLAND. SURELY THERE MUST BE A STRETCH OF BEACH THERE WE CAN LAND. AT THE VERY LEAST WE'LL SAVE THE CRATES, AND WITH ALL THOSE SHEEP WE AREN'T GOING TO STARVE.

LOW ON FUEL THE SEAFIRES REACHED LOST ISLAND, FLYING ON OVER THE SHELTERED ANCHORAGE AND THE RUINED COTTAGES OF THE FORMER INHABITANTS. AS FAR AS LANDING PLANES WENT, HOWEVER, THERE WAS NOTHING PROMISING.

NOT ENOUGH BEACH, AND EVEN THOUGH THAT HEADLAND LOOKS NICE AND FLAT, IT'S ALMOST CERTAINLY ROUGH PASTURE. LET'S TAKE A LOOK AT THE FAR SIDE OF THE ISLAND.

THE LAND ROSE TO A SERIES OF RUGGED HILLS WITH ABSOLUTELY NOWHERE TO MAKE A SAFE LANDING. BOB WAS BEGINNING TO WONDER IF IT HAD ALL BEEN A BIG MISTAKE.

UNLESS THERE'S SOMETHING THE OTHER SIDE WE'RE GOING TO HAVE TO BALE OUT AFTER ALL.

A WIDE CLEFT IN THE NEARBY ESCARPMENT OFFERED SHELTER FROM THE WIND AND INCIDENTALLY HID THE AIRCRAFT FROM THE SEA.

THIS'LL DO NICELY.

WE WERE LUCKY, SKIPPER.

THE ISLAND RECEIVED COPIOUS RAINFALL AND STREAMS GUSHED DOWN THE ESCARPMENT. IN ADDITION THERE WERE SOME SMALL CAVES.

NICE AND DRY INSIDE TO KEEP OUT OF THE WEATHER. PLENTY OF WATER.

AND FISH IN THIS POOL, BOSS. LOTS OF DRIFTWOOD FOR A FIRE AS WELL.

AS NIGHT FELL THEY ENJOYED GRILLED FISH FOR SUPPER AS THEY DISCUSSED WHAT WOULD HAPPEN.

GROWLER DIDN'T LOOK TOO BADLY DAMAGED, SKIPPER.

CAPTAIN HURST WILL GET HER OPERATIONAL AGAIN. MEANWHILE WE'LL JUST HAVE TO SIT AND WAIT. TOMORROW WE'LL EXPLORE THE REST OF THE ISLAND . . . AND HOPEFULLY ENJOY SOME ROAST MUTTON!

BOB WAS UP AND ABOUT AT FIRST LIGHT, STRETCHING STIFFLY AFTER A NONE TOO COMFORTABLE NIGHT ON THE FLOOR OF ONE OF THE CAVES.

I'LL NEED SOMETHING SOFTER TO SLEEP ON IF WE'RE GOING TO BE STUCK HERE FOR A FEW DAYS, EVEN IF IT'S ONLY A BED OF PASTURE GRASS.

NEXT MOMENT BOB GOT THE SHOCK OF HIS LIFE AS A JAPANESE FRIGATE NOSED AROUND A NEARBY HEADLAND. ACTING INSTINCTIVELY, HE DIVED FOR COVER.

GRIEF. A JAP SHIP!

WHAT'S WRONG, SKIPPER?

JOHNNY HAD CHOSEN EXACTLY THE WRONG MOMENT TO FOLLOW BOB OUT OF THE CAVE.

THEY FOUND AN EXCELLENT VANTAGE POINT OVERLOOKING THE ANCHORAGE. APART FROM THE FRIGATE, THERE WAS THE LIGHT CRUISER FROM THE DAY BEFORE, CLEARLY DAMAGED, WHILE ALONGSIDE THE WOODEN QUAY LAY A FREIGHTER AND A TRANSPORT.

I HAVE A SNEAKY FEELING THAT THIS IS THE SMALL JAP TASK FORCE THAT GERALDTON WENT OFF TO JOIN IN THE HUNT FOR.

BUT WHAT'S IT DOING HERE?

BOB BROUGHT UP HIS BINOCULARS FOR A BETTER LOOK.

THEY'RE USING INDIAN P.O.W.s TO DO THE HEAVY WORK. I DON'T KNOW WHAT THEY'RE DOING, BUT IT CERTAINLY SEEMS THEY INTEND TO BE HERE FOR A WHILE.

WHICH IS BAD NEWS FOR US!

AS THEY RETURNED TO THE BEACH BOB VOICED HIS FEARS.

IF THEY'RE HERE FOR ANY LENGTH OF TIME THEY'RE CERTAIN TO FIND US, NOT TO MENTION THE DANGER OF GROWLER SHOWING UP AND BEING CAUGHT BY SURPRISE. WE'VE GOT TO TRY AND SEND A WARNING TO THE OUTSIDE WORLD.

HOW, SKIPPER? WE'VE GOT NO RADIOS OR FUEL.

BOB HAD ALREADY CONSIDERED THAT AND THOUGHT HE MIGHT HAVE THE ANSWER. BACK AT THE AIRCRAFT HE HAD EVERY ONE CHECKED FOR REMAINING FUEL.

IF WE TRANSFER ALL THE REMAINING FUEL TO ONE CRATE IT SHOULD GIVE A RANGE OF ABOUT THREE HUNDRED MILES, ENOUGH TO REACH THE MAIN SHIPPING LANES.

I'LL GIVE IT A GO, SKIPPER.

BOB, HOWEVER, INSISTED ON DRAWING STRAWS TO CHOOSE THE PILOT, THE LONGEST ONE CLAIMING THE DUBIOUS HONOUR. IT WAS THE SQUADRON'S YOUNGEST MEMBER, PILOT OFFICER 'CORKY' CAVENDISH WHO ENDED UP WITH THE LONGEST STRAW.

LOOKS LIKE YOU'RE GOING TO SOUND THE ALARM. LET'S GET YOUR CRATE READY.

RIGHT YOU ARE, SKIPPER.

AFTER BEING WARNED TO STAY LOW AND KEEP OUT OF SIGHT OF THE OTHER SIDE OF THE ISLAND UNTIL HE WAS WELL CLEAR, THEY WATCHED THE YOUNG PILOT TAKE OFF WITH MIXED FEELINGS.

WHAT DO YOU RECKON HIS CHANCES ARE, SKIPPER?

A SHIP'S A VERY SMALL OBJECT TO FIND IN A LARGE OCEAN, JOHNNY. I WISH HIM ALL THE BEST, BUT I ALSO THINK HIS CHANCES OF SUCCEEDING, OR EVEN SURVIVING, ARE JOLLY SLIM.

BOB HOPED HIS FEARS WOULD BE PROVED WRONG.

WITH NOTHING ELSE TO DO BOB AND JOHNNY HEADED BACK TO THE VANTAGE POINT TO KEEP AN EYE ON THE INVADERS AND TO TRY AND WORK OUT WHAT THEY WERE DOING. HOWEVER, JUST AS THEY ARRIVED A SERIES OF SHOTS RANG OUT.

SHOOTING! HIT THE DECK!

DON'T TELL ME THEY'VE SPOTTED US ALREADY.

THEY NEEDN'T HAVE WORRIED. IT WAS ONLY ONE OF THE JAPANESE OFFICERS IN PURSUIT OF SOME WILD SHEEP WITH HIS RIFLE. WITH HIM WERE A GUARD AND A COUPLE OF THE P.O.W.s.

GOT IT! SEND ONE OF THE PRISONERS TO RETRIEVE THE CARCASS.

YOU, GO FETCH. SPEEDO!

HMM, THAT GULLEY'S QUITE DEEP. C'MON, JOHNNY.

THE SUDDEN APPEARANCE OF THE TWO PILOTS AT THE BOTTOM OF THE GULLEY GAVE THE INDIAN PRISONER THE SHOCK OF HIS LIFE.

BY SHIVA! WHO THE...?

KEEP IT QUIET. WE'RE ON YOUR SIDE.

THE PRISONER WAS HAVILDAR GULAM SINGH, AND AFTER GETTING OVER HIS SURPRISE HE WAS ABLE TO PROVIDE THEM WITH SOME USEFUL INFORMATION.

WE THINK THE YELLOW FACES HAVE BROUGHT US HERE TO BUILD AN AIRSTRIP. THEY WANT THE WORK FINISHED BY TOMORROW MORNING AND HAVE TOLD US WE WILL SUFFER IF IT'S NOT.

AN AIRSTRIP? ARE YOU SURE?

THE TROPICAL WATER WAS WARM ENOUGH TO RULE OUT THE RISK OF EXPOSURE. UNFORTUNATELY, IT WASN'T DEVOID OF LIFE. THE SIGHT OF A SHARK FIN CIRCLING NEARBY SPURRED CORKY INTO REACHING THE RAFT IN RECORD TIME.

NOT EXACTLY THE COMPANION I WOULD HAVE CHOSEN! WHO KNOWS HOW LONG I'M GOING TO HAVE TO WAIT UNTIL I GET PICKED UP? IF I EVER DO.

MEANWHILE, BACK ON GROWLER, CAPTAIN HURST FINALLY RECEIVED GOOD NEWS.

I CAN GIVE YOU THREE-QUARTERS AHEAD, CAP'N.

THAT WILL DO NICELY, CHIEF. THE TROUBLE IS, THE STRONG WESTERLY CURRENT'S CARRIED US ANOTHER FOUR OR FIVE HOURS AWAY FROM LOST ISLAND SINCE THE ENGINES WENT DOWN. STILL, IF WE SET OFF NOW, WE SHOULD BE THERE BY MORNING.

ON LOST ISLAND THE WORK CONTINUED THROUGH THE NIGHT AS THE POWS TOILED TO BUILD A BASIC AIRSTRIP ACROSS THE FLAT HEADLAND NEAR THE BAY. THE DARKNESS ALSO OFFERED AN OPPORTUNITY TO GET MUCH CLOSER.

LET'S WORK OUR WAY ROUND UNTIL WE'RE JUST BELOW THE HEADLAND.

THE PLOY WORKED PERFECTLY. BY THE TIME THE OTHER BARRELS JOINED THE FIRST NOBODY QUESTIONED IF THIS WAS WHERE THEY WERE SUPPOSED TO GO. GRINNING, GULAM GAVE BOB A SURREPTITIOUS THUMBS-UP.

GOOD MAN, GULAM SINGH. JOHNNY, GO FETCH THE OTHERS. WE'VE GOT WORK TO DO.

ON MY WAY, SKIPPER.

CORKY, ON THE OTHER HAND, WAS ENDURING A RATHER MORE UNPLEASANT NIGHT KEEPING A WARY EYE ON THE SHARK FINS, WHICH HAD GROWN STEADILY IN NUMBER.

THEY SAY THE BLIGHTERS NEVER SLEEP, SO PRESUMABLY THEY NEVER STOP EATING EITHER. THEY'RE PROBABLY DISCUSSING WHETHER OR NOT I'M JUST A STARTER OF THE MAIN COURSE.

TO CORKY'S AMAZEMENT THE SHIP WHICH HAD ALMOST RAN HIM DOWN TURNED OUT TO BE THE GERALDTON, SAILING TO REJOIN GROWLER AFTER A FRUITLESS SEARCH. FOR THE MOMENT, THOUGH, CORKY HAD OTHER THINGS TO WORRY ABOUT.

HELP! SHARKS!

GET SOME RIFLES UP HERE. LOWER A BOAT!

A VOLLEY OF SHOTS KEPT THE THREATENING PREDATORS AT BAY LONG ENOUGH FOR A RESCUE BOAT TO BE LAUNCHED.

THERE HE IS, STRAIGHT AHEAD!

AND STILL IN ONE PIECE.

THE COMMANDER IN CHARGE OF THE GERALDTON WAS ASTOUNDED TO LEARN THAT CORKY WAS ONE OF THE FLIERS FROM GROWLER, AND EVEN MORE SO WHEN HE LEARNT ABOUT THE JAP PRESENCE ON LOST ISLAND.

WE'LL SET COURSE FOR LOST ISLAND, FULL SPEED AHEAD. YOU'LL GET A WARM BUNK FOR THE NIGHT. YOU DESERVE IT.

I'M LOOKING FORWARD TO IT, AND THAT'S A FACT.

THE REASON FOR THE FLURRY OF ACTIVITY BECAME CLEAR AS A FLIGHT OF LONG RANGE MITSUBISHI BOMBERS, CODENAMED "NELL" BY THE ALLIES, FLEW IN FROM THE NORTH-EAST AND PREPARED TO LAND ON THE ROUGH BUT SERVICEABLE AIRSTRIP THAT HAD BEEN LAID OUT ACROSS THE HEADLAND.

THEY'VE GOT FUEL, BOMBS AND FRESH CREWS WAITING. WHERE DO THEY GO FROM HERE?

SOUTH AFRICA'S JUST FIFTEEN HUNDRED MILES AWAY. THE NELLS CAN MAKE A ROUND TRIP OF THREE THOUSAND MILES WITH PLENTY TO SPARE. MY GUESS IS THEY'RE PLANNING TO BOMB CAPE TOWN AND PERHAPS DURBAN. COME ON, WE'VE GOT THE ONLY WEAPONS TO STOP THEM . . . THE SEAFIRES.

SUDDENLY ONE OF THE INCOMING BOMBERS MAKES A WIDER APPROACH THAN THE OTHERS, BRINGING IT STRAIGHT OVER BOB AND JOHNNY.

LOOK DOWN THERE!

HECK!

WE'VE BEEN RUMBLED!

IT WAS OBVIOUS THEY HAD BEEN SEEN AND THERE WAS ONLY ONE COURSE OF ACTION.

DUMP THE BARREL. RUN FOR IT!

ALERT THE GROUND. WARN THEM OF INTRUDERS!

THE NEWS WAS FLASHED TO THE GROUND AND ACTED UPON IMMEDIATELY BY THE JAPANESE.

AIRCRAFT REPORTS INTRUDERS BEYOND THE HEADLAND. SQUAD THREE, COME WITH ME. SPEEDO!

THEY'VE BEEN SPOTTED.

THE PURSUIT PARTY QUICKLY FOUND THE ABANDONED BARREL AND GAVE CHASE.

THEY WENT THIS WAY! AFTER THEM!

YES, CAPTAIN-SAN!

MEANWHILE THE BOMBERS WERE BEING FUELLED AND ARMED AT A FEVERISH RATE, THEIR CREWS REPLACED BY FRESH ONES WHO HAD TRAVELLED TO THE ISLAND ON BOARD THE TRANSPORT SHIP.

BY NIGHTFALL, CAPE TOWN WILL BE ABLAZE, AND TOMORROW DURBAN!

THIS IS TERRIBLE.

GULAM HAD PICKED UP ENOUGH JAPANESE DURING HIS TIME IN CAPTIVITY TO UNDERSTAND WHAT WAS BEING SAID.

ACROSS THE ISLAND BOB AND JOHNNY WERE RUNNING FOR THEIR LIVES.

THERE THEY GO!

TAKE COVER!

TOO RIGHT, SKIPPER!

THEY REACHED THE BEACH AND RAN TOWARDS THEIR WAITING AIRCRAFT, WHICH HAD ALL BEEN FUELLED UP.

JAPS AFTER US! GET READY TO SCRAMBLE!

AT ONCE, SIR!

THE ENGINES HAD ALREADY BEEN WARMED UP, WHICH WAS JUST AS WELL, BECAUSE OTHERWISE THERE WOULD NEVER HAVE BEEN TIME.

BY SHINTO. FIGHTER AIRCRAFT!

GOT TO GET AIRBORNE FAST.

THE SEAFIRES ROARED INTO THE AIR THROUGH A HAIL OF GUNFIRE.

STOP THEM! FIRE!

JUST SMALL-ARMS FIRE. NOT ENOUGH TO DO ANY REAL DAMAGE, I HOPE.

58

THE JAPANESE GUARDS, THEIR NUMBER GREATLY REDUCED BY THE ABSENCE OF THOSE WHO HAD GONE AFTER BOB AND JOHNNY, WERE STARING STUNNED AT THE SCENE OF DESTRUCTION WHEN GULAM AND HIS FELLOW PRISONERS LAUNCHED AN ATTACK ON THEM.

KILL THE YELLOW FACES!

WHAT THE . . . YEUURGH!

SEEING WHAT WAS HAPPENING, BOB AND JOHNNY MADE ANOTHER PASS, THIS TIME TARGETING JAPS ON THE GROUND TO HELP THE INDIANS.

YOUR TURN TO BE ON THE RECEIVING END, JAP!

THANK YOU, MY FRIENDS. GRAB THEIR GUNS!

AAARGH!

AIEE!

SUDDENLY BOB REALISED THAT JOHNNY WAS POINTING MADLY OUT TO SEA, WHERE A WELCOME SIGHT WAS APPROACHING.

GLORY BE. IT'S GROWLER!

BOB LED HIS PLANES IN TO LAND ON GROWLER, BUT HE HAD NO INTENTION OF STAYING LONG.

WE CAN PICK UP SOME BOMBS AND HIT THE SHIPS BEFORE THEY CAN ESCAPE THE ANCHORAGE.

FOR THE JAPS THE LAST STRAW WAS THE APPEARANCE OF SEVERAL MORE SHIPS, ALL CONVERGING ON LOST ISLAND IN RESPONSE TO CALLS FOR THE GERALDTON. THE SURVIVORS ABANDONED THEIR POSITIONS AND FLED.

AIEE!

LET THEM GO. THEY CAN BE ROUNDED UP LATER.

RUN!

FOR THE INDIANS THERE WAS THE ADDED EXHILARATION OF NO LONGER BEING PRISONERS OF THE JAPANESE. A JUBILANT GULAM WAVED TO THE SEAFIRES AS THEY FLEW OVER ON THEIR RETURN FLIGHT TO GROWLER. BOB LOOKED DOWN AND SMILED.

ALL'S WELL THAT ENDS WELL, THANKS TO THE CASTAWAY SQUADRON — WE HAD SOME HELP, THOUGH!

WELL DONE, MY FRIENDS!

ON SALE NOW!

No. 4107
£1.25
Commando
FOR ACTION AND ADVENTURE

OSCAR'S ARMY

No. 4109
£1.25
Commando
FOR ACTION AND ADVENTURE

SPLIT-SECOND TIMING

No. 4110
£1.25
Commando
FOR ACTION AND ADVENTURE

DEATH DUEL

www.commandomag.com

CONTACT DETAILS By post: The Commando, D.C. Thomson & Co., Ltd, 2 Albert Square Dundee DD1 9QJ
email: editor@commandomag.com
phone: **01382 223131**

PROMOTIONS promotions@dcthomson.co.uk
SUBSCRIPTIONS subscriptions@dcthomson.co.uk
SYNDICATION syndication@dcthomson.co.uk
CIRCULATION circulation@dcthomson.co.uk

ADVERTISING SALES
email: robin@o2o.co.uk
020 7321 0701
or
01372 802 300

LICENSING
start.licensing@btinternet.com

recycle
When you have finished with
this magazine please recycle it.

COMPETITION RULES Employees of D.C. Thomson and their families are not eligible for prizes. The Editor's decision is final and no correspondence will be entered into.

Printed and Published in Great Britain by D.C. Thomson & Co., Ltd., 185 Fleet Street, London EC4A 2HS.
© D.C. Thomson & Co., Ltd., 2008